Q2

Cambridge English Readers

Level Two

SUP

BRIAN TOMLINSON

CAMBRIDGE
UNIVERSITY PRESS

PUBLISHED BY THE PRESS SYNDICATE OF THE UNIVERSITY OF CAMBRIDGE, UNITED KINGDOM
The Pitt Building, Trumpington Street, Cambridge CB2 1RP

CAMBRIDGE UNIVERSITY PRESS
The Edinburgh Building, Cambridge CB2 2RU, United Kingdom
40 West 20th Street, New York, NY 10011-4211, USA
10 Stamford Road, Oakleigh, Melbourne 3166, Australia

Printed in the United Kingdom at the University Press, Cambridge

CHE

A storm in the desert

The desert from the night sky

The Americans see the light

Superbird flies low over the desert

Good morning. Welcome to Radio News Today.

Fifty years ago Superbird crashed into a hill in a desert. Well, you know that already, don't you? And you thought five people died. Ford, Stone, Sands, Bridges and Mount. But only four people died. Yes, that's right. Four people, not five! Mount came back. She is here today, aged 75.

This morning I went to see Mount. I talked to her about the crash in the desert.

Hello, Mount. It's nice to see you. How are you?

I'm OK. I'm happy to be here. Feeling a little old maybe. It's nice to talk to somebody.

Today it's July 4th, fifty years since the crash in the desert.

Is it really? Fifty years today?

Can you tell us what happened?

Yes, I can. I can tell you now. For fifty years I've kept quiet. They told me to say nothing. But today they said I can speak to you.

OK. Mount, what happened on that night fifty years ago?

A lot happened. We were flying at night. We were taking photos of lights. At first there were lots of lights below us. Lots of lights together. Cities of lights. But then it was dark. There were no lights below us at all. And then there was a terrible noise. And a great light in the sky. Something hit us. We were so afraid.

What did you do?

We tried the radio. Nothing. Then our lights went out. We were in the dark. And there was no noise. Everything was very quiet because Superbird's engines weren't working. Ford tried to bring Superbird down in the desert.

Ford tried to land the plane on a hill?

No, no. On the sand. There was soft sand everywhere. We landed on the sand. But the plane didn't stop. We hit the sand again and again. Once, twice, three times. Then we hit the hill.

And all the men died?

No. Not then. Not at once. Ford and Stone died when we hit the hill. Sands was hurt; he couldn't move. But Bridges was OK. He kept saying, "I'm OK, I'm OK."

What about you?

I was all right too. I moved my arms, I moved my legs. Nothing hurt. I was OK. I looked out of the window. Nothing. There were no lights. Everything was black. Bridges took my hand and he said, "Let's go outside. Let's get away from Superbird before they come."

So you did? You went outside?

I said, "What about Sands?"

Sands heard me and he said, "You must go. Go now before they come."

Did you go then?

Yes. We gave Sands a drink and then we left him on the floor of the plane. We opened the door and we jumped out. It was a long way down. But the sand was soft. We walked down the hill, Bridges and I, holding hands. Then we saw lights on the road coming near us fast. Lots of bright lights and a lot of noise.

What were they? Cars? Planes? Lorries?

We didn't know. We could only see the lights. We got down flat on the sand. We wanted the lights to go on past us, but they stopped near the hill. Then there were lots of people and a lot more noise – people shouting, people shouting back. They put a bright light on Superbird. I could see Sands looking out of the window.

Did they see you?

No. They were all looking at Superbird. Then they ran. A lot of people ran up the hill. Some of them went inside Superbird. I could hear guns. Then I heard Sands shouting, screaming. They shot him many times. Then suddenly everything was quiet.

What about you? Did you have guns?

No. We had nothing. We lay in the sand and watched from

the dark. Then they came out of Superbird. They were carrying bags. Three bags. Ford, Stone and Sands. Then some of the lights went away along the road, taking the bags. But some of the lights stayed near the hill. They were watching Superbird but they didn't see us.

What did you do then?

Nothing. We just waited there in the dark, holding hands. We waited for a long time. Then lights came from the dark with more people and lots of noise. They put Superbird on a very big lorry and they drove it away very slowly, into the dark. Then it was very quiet. There were a few people and some lights, but very little noise.

Could you see the people?

We were a long way away. But we could see some of them sitting under the lights. They looked very big. We were afraid but we moved nearer the lights to look at the people. We moved very slowly along the sand.

What did the people look like? Did they look like us?

No. Not at all. They were very tall. They had brown hair all over their heads and they had something strange in the middle of their faces. Like our noses but much bigger. And some had things over their eyes, things which came from their ears. Some had hair on their faces too.

Were they wearing clothes?

Yes, they were wearing clothes, brown clothes. But not like ours. The clothes covered their bodies, they covered their arms, their legs and even the tops of their heads. And they had guns. But one of the people was different. It had very long yellow hair and you could see its legs. And it didn't have a gun. It was sitting on a chair and it was writing. A very big brown-haired person was standing and talking to it.

Superbird crashes into a hill in a storm

Lights come across the desert towards Superbird

The lights are on Superbird as they carry out Ford, Stone and Sands

They put Superbird onto a big lorry

Could you hear the brown haired person? What was it saying?

I could hear it but the sounds were strange. The words were not the same as ours.

Could you understand anything?

No. The brown-haired one was very loud. It kept shouting. The yellow-haired person kept on saying something like "sir". Again and again. We were standing still in the dark when suddenly there was a very loud noise, and the sky was full of light. The people saw us and started shouting at us. Then they started shooting at us with their guns. We ran back into the dark very fast. They ran after us, shooting all the time. Now the sky was dark again and I ran up the hill. When I got to the top of the hill, I lay down on the ground.

Was Bridges with you?

No. Bridges didn't run up the hill. He ran the other way, into the desert. I saw him when the sky was full of light again. They saw him too. They shot him four or five times. He fell down and they shot him again. They all ran to Bridges. Then it became dark again. And very quiet. Their lights were on his body and one of them said something like, "No blood." And the others all said something like, "Wow!"

Did they find you?

No. They looked for me everywhere with their lights, but they didn't come up the hill. After a long time they went back to their cars and some of the cars drove away. Then I fell asleep.

How long did you sleep?

I don't know. But when I woke up the sky was not so dark. I could see a big red light, a long way away. Most of the people were sleeping in their cars. But two of them were standing and looking at the red light.

Did they see you?

No. It was still dark on the hill. I went over the top of the hill and down the other side. Then I ran away from the red light in the sky. Soon it started to get lighter and lighter. The sky was changing from black to blue. I kept running and running, and then I saw a house. When I got near to the house I saw lots of small people. They were all white, except one which was black, and they had four legs. They were eating something green in the sand. When they saw me they made strange noises and ran away. I kept running too, running to the house.

Why? Why didn't you run the other way, away from the house?

I don't know. I was running away from the light to the house. It was getting lighter and soon the sky was blue and the sun was yellow. When I got to the house, I looked in an open window and I could see one of the big people. It was one of the yellow-haired people. This one had no clothes on and it was sitting in water. Its body was wet and very white. It was singing.

Did it see you?

Not at first. But then another person with four legs suddenly ran at me. This one was small and brown, and it had long hair. It made a very loud noise and then it tried to bite my leg. The person in the water looked up and saw me at the window. It screamed very loudly and I screamed very loudly too. The four-legged person stopped trying to bite me and ran away. Then the yellow-haired person and I stopped screaming and we smiled. I smiled at the yellow-haired person and it smiled at me. We smiled at each other for a long time.

Was it still in the water?

Yes, it was. But then it got out of the water. It put on a white coat and it came outside the house to meet me. We looked at each other for a long time and then it took my hand. Its hand was still wet but it was soft like Bridges' hand the night before. We held hands and then we went inside the house.

What happened in the house?

The four-legged person came back. The yellow-haired person spoke to it quietly and then it sat down by my feet and started to clean my hand with its tongue.

Did they speak to you?

The four-legged one did, but the yellow-haired one said nothing. It just smiled and held my hand. Then it gave me something to eat, some dry brown things in white water. It put some white sand on top and smiled. I ate the food and smiled too.

What happened then?

The yellow-haired one took me into another room and put me into a bed. When I was lying down with my head on something soft and white, it kissed me. Then it left the room and the four-legged person got onto the bed and went to sleep next to me. When I woke up, the yellow-haired one was standing by the bed, smiling. It was wearing a long red thing, but I could see its legs. It gave me a newspaper. There were lots of words, which I couldn't understand, but there were also two photos. One photo was of Superbird on the hill. The other one was of Bridges and myself with a big light behind us in the sky. The yellow-haired person looked at my photo and then looked at me. Again she smiled.

What about the other people? What did they do?

There were no other people in the house. Just the two of them. There were lots of small people outside, but there were no other people in the house. Once I heard a car, and voices that came and then went away. For three days I stayed in bed, often with the four-legged person lying next to me. Every night the yellow-haired person kissed me and then went away. Every morning when I woke up it was standing by my bed, smiling.

Soldiers look for Mount in the desert

Soldiers watch the red light grow bigger in the sky

The 'small people' run away

The yellow-haired person sings in the bath

What happened after three days?

I woke up in the morning. The yellow-haired person was standing by my bed. It kissed me and then held my hand. I saw then that it had only five fingers on each hand. It pulled me carefully out of the bed and took me into another room. There were four very big brown-haired people in this room, sitting on chairs. They all had guns, but they smiled at me and I smiled back. They took me out and put me in the back of a car with the yellow-haired person. She held my hand while one of the brown-haired people put something over my eyes so that I couldn't see. Everything was dark again. I could hear the four-legged person making a lot of noise.

Where did they take you?

I don't know. When the car stopped somebody kissed me and got out of the car. Then the car moved again just a little way. When it stopped this time somebody took my hand and pulled me out of the car. We walked for about two hundred metres and then stopped. They took the thing off my eyes and I could see that I was in a room. It was a nice room – very big and colourful. There were three brown-haired people there. They smiled at me and then we all sat down at a table.

You had a meal?

No. They showed me a photo of Superbird taken after the crash, and they gave me a pen. At first I didn't know what they wanted me to do, so I just took the pen and smiled at the people. Then one of them started drawing Superbird with a pen on a piece of paper. Suddenly I knew what to do. I drew a picture of Superbird as it was before the crash. Then they all smiled too.

The yellow-haired person smiles at Mount

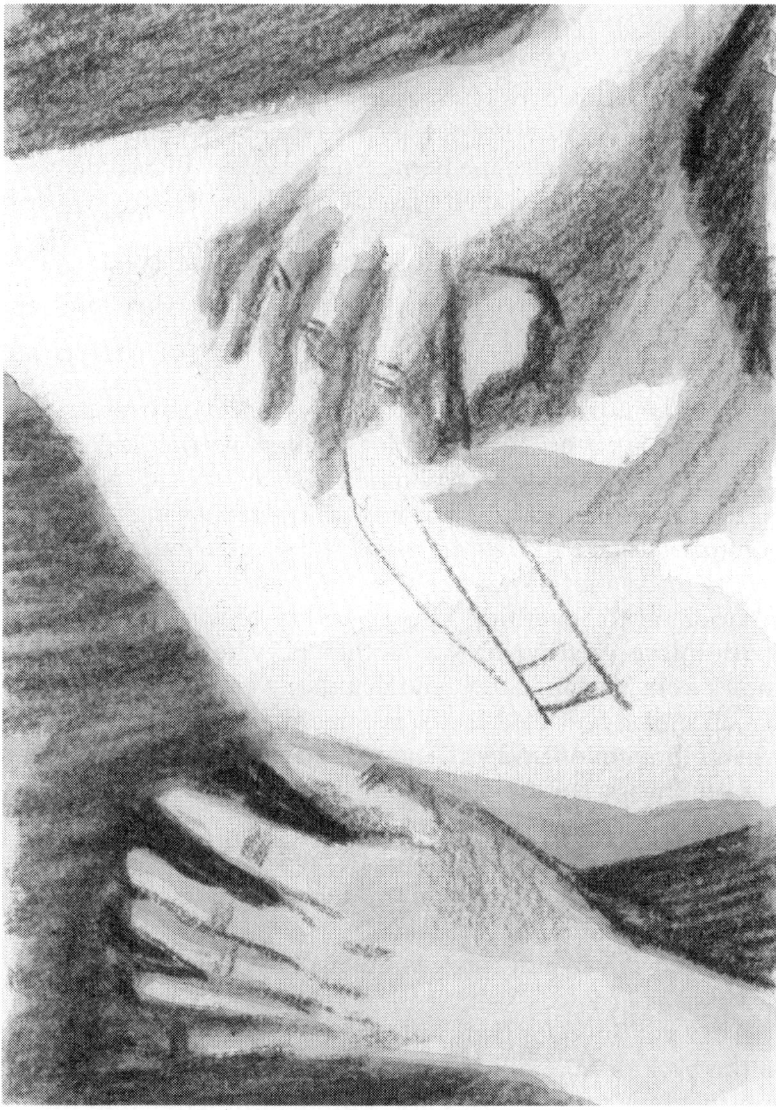

Mount draws Superbird

How long did you stay there?

A long time. Maybe nine months. They taught me their language. It's called English. And I taught some of them our language too. Soon we could speak to each other and they told me they wanted to take me home. So every day I helped them to re-build Superbird and then I taught them how to fly it.

Where did you fly to?

We only flew at night. Just up into the dark sky and back again. And they always put something over my eyes until we were in the plane.

So tell us. How did you get back here?

One night, the yellow-haired person came to my room with the four-legged person and a lot of brown-haired people. It kissed me while they took a photo. It looked very sad and then it started to cry. I asked it why it was crying, but it didn't speak. It just turned round and left the room, still crying. The four-legged person made a lot of noise as they put something over my eyes and took me to Superbird. There were two brown-haired people in the plane wearing brown clothes. They told me that their names were Sam and Steve, and that they were taking me home. We all smiled and held hands as Superbird took off. I was sad when I thought of Bridges. And of Ford, Stone and Sands. But I was very happy because I was going home.

What happened when you got back here?

They told me to land the plane in a desert at night. So I landed it in the middle of the Dark Desert.

What happened when you landed?

I smiled at Sam and Steve, but they didn't smile at me.

What did they do?

They got out their guns and told me to get into the Supercar in the back of Superbird. They opened the door of the plane, and then got into the back seat of Supercar. They told me to drive the car off the plane and on to the desert. Then they told me to drive towards the hills. It was very dark, but sometimes with lightning in the sky, just like the night when we crashed on Earth nine months before. They told me to drive without lights; so I drove very slowly.

Were you afraid?

No. It was very easy in the dark to start the Hiss machine. The brown-haired people didn't know about that. There was a small noise as the gas came out. They screamed and then they were dead.

What about you?

I was all right. The gas we used kills other people, but it doesn't hurt us. I put the car lights on, and then I drove back to Superbird. I put all the plane lights on and waited for somebody to come. Soon a plane landed and four soldiers ran towards me with guns. I stood in the light and waved my arms. Somebody shot at me but didn't hit me. Then somebody shouted, "Stop shooting! It's Mount. She's come back."

But why did they tell us you were dead? Where did you go?

They took me to a hospital and they asked me questions. Every day for six months they asked me questions. They wanted to know all about the Earth people. I told them everything. Just like I'm telling you. Then they left me there for all these years. I grew old in a small room, with a soldier outside the door. And then today they opened the door, and I walked out into the garden. And you were sitting there, smiling at me.

Have they told you the news? This morning Superbirds 2, 3, 4, 5 and 6 took off for Earth. This is a great day.

Is that right? Then it's a great day for me too.

Mount smiled, shook hands with me and went back to her room.

Mount tells her story

Superbirds 2, 3, 4, 5 and 6 fly to Earth